These are poems that
neme by phone
unusual but not
lamb beside, / Sl
ems draw the rea
feeling, thinking? The unique character of what a friend of mine called "languageness" makes for powerful images and seductive syntax. As I read, I find myself in Asia: "The steam of noodles in their bowls / As though a grand aquarium / Flowing alive in Saigon streets." And then we are with a child in apparent danger as we read: "Dear parents—far away! / It's just another carnival. / It's just another day." There are constant surprises linguistically and spiritually. Indeed, these intimate and careful poems have a deep spiritual well that enables the poet to drift toward the edge and, at the same time, respect the abyss: "And assume her, that she stands, full moon-posed, / The referent—one hand resting upon / The mature animal in four colors, / The other of liquid silver extends / To paradise."

MICHAEL POAGE
Fulbright Professor of English Literature and Usage,
Walailak University, Thailand,
author of *An Incident That Might Lead to Something*

Alex Van Huynh's first collection takes us into the deep inquiries of a mind fully engaged with both the known and unknowable. Informed by mythology, history, religion, and science, these poems explore "the whole world in miniature," where the "pores of the earth pull beneath the sands," as well as the vast expanses of sky and sea, where "drifting things must come naked." Huynh's subjects are often reminded "our condition is temporary," but he is a voice who is establishing a permanent place for himself in American poetry.

HAYLEY MITCHELL HAUGEN
editor-in-chief of *Sheila-Na-Gig*, author of *The Blue Wife Poems*

Curious, erudite, and darkly whimsical, the very best work of Dr. Alex Van Huynh's poetry collection, *Inquiry*, tackles the harrowing without being hopeless.

KATRINA AGBAYANI
associate editor at *Acta Victoriana*

A towering achievement of cultural synthesis and literary alchemy, rendered in poetry that seems summoned out of a mythic past, full of magic. Alex Van Huynh, biologist by training but a scholar of, well, *everything*, announces early in this volume

> *I will extend in fullness*
> *Until that choice is made of light—*
> *The colors coalesce to white,*
> *And by my right, I will to see*
> *What massiveness it brings to be!*

Massiveness is the right description for this world-embodying work, but while intellectually rigorous and exhilarating, it is never ponderous, buoyed by the musicality of Huynh's lyrical language, which demands to be read aloud, shamelessly replete with iambs and occasional rhymes. His love of words is infectious (who else could use *sphexish* so naturally, so unpretentiously?) So is his love of "this natural space," containing birds and trees as well as "human girls with half their clothes / And happy from the night." (Though less romantically, he also notes how our online lives have replaced relationships with "Just usernames–sex in hand.")

In his closing poem, he poses the big question:

> *The first burn of the story fades*
> *And just its ashy words are left to gather—*
> *Their drifts to tell what only was once*
> *And ask what man has to give.*

What Huynh has to give is this book, and it is a compelling response.

LARRY W. MOORE
publisher of Broadstone Books

Inquiry

by Alex Van Huynh

Inquiry

©2023 by Alex Van Huynh

Fernwood Press
Newberg, Oregon
www.fernwoodpress.com

All rights reserved. No part may be reproduced for any commercial purpose by any method without permission in writing from the copyright holder.

Printed in the United States of America

Cover and page design: Mareesa Fawver Moss
Cover photo: Ashleigh Joy Photography

ISBN 978-1-59498-107-4

Table of Contents

Introduction 9
Part I: I ask of you 15
   Good morning fairgrounds! 16
   My credentials 17
   Sunflowers 18
   Father Hux 19
   Open window 20
   Polenka 21
   The Paxtons 22
   Pratzen Heights 23
   American plastic 24
   Breslau's crowds 25
   Avatar 26
   New *Hamamelis* 28
   Nature at her table 30
   Empty church 32

Part II: In this natural space 33
   Those fierce macaws 34
   Mortal light 35
   October fog 36

A hidden green 37
Extended blue 38
Blackened boughs 39
Ring-cupped oak 40
Throbbing mayapple 41
Little figures 42
The vivid procession 43
Thoughts at large 44
To the little chickadee 45
Seabright 46
The juniper 47
A Mid-Atlantic Easter 48
Ruby-throated hummingbird 49
The chemical estate 50
How quiet 51
Southern seas 52
Origin 53

Part III: What we may carry 55
The little man 56
Come rave! 57
The sorry boy from Watertown 58
On the rim 59
The bathroom 60
Twilit town 61
Annalight 62
Poses as a girl 63
Which ward? 64
Another day of carnival 65
Documented 66
A sunlit moment 67
As do their dreamers 68
In death or a woman 69
Old professor 70

Silver cay 71
Pipe and box 72
Concrescence 73
Starship girl 74
The young poet 75

Part IV: Or whom we love 77
I call you mistress, Lesvos 78
Upon the Monmouth 79
Inflection 80
The west fields 81
Two things 82
Beauty in blue and beauty in white 83
Boardwalk dreams 84
Dublin asks 85
A boy named Holly 86
The sunlit lord 87
That awful cutter 88
Double her 89
Lilith 90
Clementine Quixotestein 91
Abomination 92
Cassidy! 93
A fairy girl 94

Part V: From that other world 97
Private Jacob 98
A protean place 99
City in chrome 100
Arianrhod 101
The exhibit 102
Skylines in parallax 103
Paperman 104
Leopold and Lotty 105
The Light Man 106

A glitch	107
The holy traps	108
Low-hanging sun	110
That great black glass	111
My accolades	112
What man has to give	113

References	115
Acknowledgments	117
Title Index	119
First Line Index	123

Introduction

It has been 2,500 years since Parmenides authored the fragments of his only surviving work, the poem *On Nature*.[1] As I was preparing this collection, between the wild pullings that the variegated themes within the poetry you are about to read had on my attention, I found my thoughts continuously returning to an early childhood memory. One whose Eleatic echo I would only later appreciate, this memory was of a question I used to ask myself. I cannot remember how old I was exactly nor, like the nature of a dream, the specific circumstances around its beginnings, but it must have been an early product of my quite average suburban American upbringing and my innate imaginative inquisitiveness that would later lead me into a career of scholarship. The hypothetical went something like this: "If there was no God, would there be nothing? Would there not even be nothing?" It was as what James Joyce said was "nothing, nothing or less than nothing."[2] Concentrating on this and its slight variations, I would eventually produce a strong reaction in myself—a strange feeling at once physical and mental. The impression was unpleasantly disorienting, and as a child, its quiddity seemed to evade all description and thus the possibility for its communication to others or complete comprehension in myself. To this point, little has changed in the twenty-odd years since. Today, I refer to it as a sort of *spinal feeling*. It felt deep rooted, in the body axis itself, like a shock in the reflex arcs. It was also incredibly fleeting, as instantaneous as an experience could be and still be called such. Faced with pure incomprehensibility and by implication one of the eternal truths that is our limitations, whether by nature or by ego, the contents of the flash were impossible to remember exactly even just a few moments afterward. So I would repeat the exercise, letting the same terrible thing briefly illuminate itself, always to disappear instanter. There are ways to touch the spirit, and for me, this was one of them. In asking this question, I do not believe I ever aimed to actually answer it—that was not the point. I did it simply to produce the sensation, which perhaps, as I reflect on it today, was the answer in itself.

Questions are extraordinarily important to the human enterprise and have been for thousands of years. "Those who have formulated the world's problems have more often deserved the name 'philosopher' than those who have settled them."[3] In the West, the origins of systematic questioning can be traced back to the Socratic *elenchus*. In the Platonic dialogues, beginning with the "What is F-ness?" Socrates would continue with lines of questions to the ostensibly wise man.[4] Commonly defined as a request for information,[5] a more formal treatment by Cohen identifies the basic question as a "propositional function," the correct answer to which is a true proposition of said function.[3] However, because questions come in a variety of forms, a single descriptor is difficult to accept. Beyond the simple propositional function, there are questions lacking an interrogative (i.e. yes-or-no), questions with multiple answers (indeterminate), questions without answers (invalid), and apparent questions that cannot be properly defined as questions at all (ambiguous).[3]

Beyond its philosophical and syntactical deconstruction, the question has been formalized into various hierarchies of cognition,[6] one of the most well known being Bloom's Taxonomy,[7] which increasingly includes: abstraction, knowledge, comprehension, application, analysis, synthesis, and evaluation. Within this framework, the inquirer, whether it be the psychologist or the educational instructor, has a specific purpose for their questioning beyond the simple act of seeking answers—namely, to elicit higher level cognitive processes in the subject or student.[6, 8] In psychotherapy, it is often the indeterminate question that is most important. Here the question takes the place of the statement, i.e. simple advice, enabling the patient instead to discover that they already know the solution and can make the right decisions for themselves.[9, 10] In education, the teacher is "a professional question maker."[11] Again, the kinds of questions and their overall sequence as it leads the student toward understanding is what is paramount. "It is important that teachers' questions should not be viewed as an end in themselves. They are a means to an end—producing desired changes in student behavior."[6] This is especially interesting as it relates to the sciences. All of science stems from asking questions—this is what the discipline trains its very scientists to do.[12] As a scientist and educator myself, I teach students to ask questions by asking questions.

In the East, the question often takes a central role in the spiritual life. Among the various schools of Zen Buddhism, there is the koan (Ch'an: *kung-an*, Sŏn: *kongan*, Zen: *kōan*). A koan is usually defined, albeit somewhat simplistically, as a "paradox" or "nonsensical question." Most notably in the Rinzai school, koans are used in the practice of contemplating "critical phrases" (*watō*), where answers to proposed questions are the objects of meditation until the student achieves *satori* or a state of sudden awakening. In literary terms, koans are comprised of root cases or patriarchal records (*ku-tsu*) once raised in question to a Ch'an master and his subsequent commentary (*yü-lu*).[13] In this way, they are similar in initial presentation to the Socratic *elenchus*. However, in practice, instead of leading one through a series of logical deductions, in seeking their explanations koans are meant to produce "frustration and final abandonment or transcendence of such merely intellectual approaches."[13] For example, take the famous "Tung-Shan's Three Pounds of Flax," where Tung-Shan is weighing out flax in the temple storeroom:

> *A monk asked Tung-Shan, "What is Buddha?"*
> *Tung-Shan said, "Three pounds of flax."*[14]

Secondary (and even tertiary) questions and commentary by Zen authorities on these discourses comprise many koan collections today (e.g. Blue Cliff Collection, Gateless Barrier). Thus, questions of the invalid type can be of the highest spiritual importance. It is ultimately the question that, as Rinazi master Asahina Sōgen remarks of koans, "express[es] the enlightened state completely."[15]

What then do questions have to do with poetry? The White Queen tells Alice a "lovely riddle—all in poetry—all about fishes."[16] The relationship between poetry and questions runs deep. Robert Graves cites what Alun Lewis called "the single poetic theme of Life and Death—the question of what survives of the beloved."[17] According to Graves, "perfect faithfulness to the theme affects the reader of a poem with a strange feeling, between delight and horror."[17] This aspect of what Graves calls "true poetry" has its roots in the inextricable connection between poetry and the question. In *The White Goddess,* Graves explores the questions and riddles found in the early bardic poetry of Wales and Ireland such as *Cad Goddeu* and *Hanes Taliesen.* Graves submits his analyses of these and other poems along with much additional anthropological discussion as evidence for widespread goddess worship during Bronze Age Europe, North Africa, and Asia Minor. It is this tripartite goddess, the "more-than-muse," which the poet must celebrate and whose history is veiled in poetic riddle.[17,18]

St. John of the Cross remarked that "enough has been said to effect all that is needed."[19] Why then do we go on questioning, looking for answers that will satisfy our individual lives or perhaps illuminate, even partially, whatever ultimate truths there may be? I believe that this is the great pastime. Beyond that pretense of purpose in the question, we ask aimlessly, just as the poem is its own end. They are not signs but the referent itself. It is as when Faust asks Helen:

> *Why puzzle, why insist? Our unique role*
> *Bids us exist; one moment means the whole.*[20]

Eventually, the question I played with as a child changed for me. Today, it carries all of its philosophy, but its gravity is gone. The feeling that used to overwhelm me is unreachable to me now. Occasionally, I still try to meditate on it, to feel for that horrible mystery, but I cannot find it. Like Proust, I am left with just the mnemonic fact of my tea and madeleine, the unfolding world, or in my case, the appalling absence thereof, beyond them has utterly withdrawn.[21] Poetry is a relationship between the poet and the reader—what Graves called that "tripled togetherness of you with me."[17] The poems in this book are my questions. Perhaps they are my way to pose that question I used to love but can no longer properly ask myself. They come from my experiences and my thoughts, but insofar as they are of that single poetic theme, they are yours and all the world's as well. I hope that, in them, we can ask together as we have always asked and will be asking forever.

> *I ask of you*
> *In this natural space*
> *What we may carry*
> *Or whom we love*
> *From that other world*

Part I: I ask of you

Good morning fairgrounds!

Good morning fairgrounds! Silent fog
Such that white London Town away
Should bear forth from its misty womb
Some new world, long and lean in line—
What posts are past the water-veil?
All occidental trees but one
And the true Tolstoyan pillar
Alone, falling, fast, and midnight—

Atlas and axis aching at the drums,
Dark harps in the teeth, songs for the sleepless
Ordeal—to chase those sourceless pipes away—
Awake! A fresh house of modernity—
Cool rooms wash o'er the skull now forgotten
From the painkillers, dead parents walking,
And in the suburban fallout is played
A right relief upon mind's ivories.

My credentials

To say something of my credentials?
I walk past the university rows,
My eyes begging at those far-off young smiles—
High legs daring to autumn, rosy cheeks
As if given? Purchased in decision?
It is paid in full—in father! For what?
Recurring, worrying of wives and race
When jungles of a Vietnam encroach
On the lawns—foreign sons forsaken for
Regality on the glassy highwalks,
All layered in a sort of cellophane—
Invisible images for the flies
To fill as glassware, see it fire with eyes
Cut lidless, and earth denied her rolling.
Those are my papers. Are you assured?

Sunflowers

To fell a like man on even matters—
What else could be more right than that?
Queer it is as an automatic thing,
That bang. So tell it so! A tale
Broken, let run forever to that end
Would so shiver the little parts
That a brief respite in rock, one's own ground,
Cautions: "It's only up from here!"

A giggle from the edges—such is man!
A wash of some great scene from greater plan—
As space, sunflowers across glassy spans.

Father Hux

Oh, Father Hux! I have quite forgotten
What thing he so desperately impressed
On me, my babe—but what blackest friar
He was! And now? Back to the Prince's Dock
No doubt, and some beautiful man with more!
If only I had known of what I won't
And not been not particular these years—
Last, a life made of cities and birthdays—
E'er in and out of some fraternity
Where, though I can do no right, know nothing,
But on the personalities get by,
Looking—just skeletons beneath the skirts
Lifted by all sorts of terrible hands,
Barely in the dark so as not to glimpse
Through the palm-holes, their tumultuous rift.
The folds of my humanity coming
In the unspeaking fastness of the craft—
A purpleness sets to the world's feeling—
Below, descending space with my musings.

I will extend in fullness
Until that choice is made of light—
The colors coalesce to white,
And by my right, I will to see
What massiveness it brings to be!

Open window

Breakfast
As if someone made it interrupted—
Bare feet press on the boards in normal light,
Its inclined appearance of the rooms
So familiar they seem to be moving
At the will to move to where it will.

The noise
Upstairs and unbelievable, it was
That past the shapes and patterns, memories
Forgotten and made new, he was frightened.
No one had a bedroom, but inside it—
Open window, broken spirit—*death*.

Rosewood
Under the glass, small warps of divine sight
With floor-dust his mother would never clean
Must have seen the demiurgic act—who
Like a bird, a breeze, or boy could it be
When none exist—no nature to man?

Question
Of the observable fact—Looking out
And seeing himself clearer in the world,
The sudden naked sense—that thinnest fair
Partition is gone! Ink-eyes circling,
Black tears to the static, say likeness.

Polenka

Young boys with their small papers, criminal,
And then quaternary man's wide eye sees
All things in sight are slipping—
Living, the great delirium.

The world loosened and permitted its gyre,
Poor Polenka—dizzying ringing for
The only theme—a student and a whore
By candlelight comfort one another
In what ways but those eternal and drawn
Down by some unknowing progenitor,
Rising, rushing, racing, and welling up
Into each, face forever—crystallin
Reflections diving deep, planet printers,
To that terrible laughing or weeping?
It's for one man alone to hear and do—
Siberia! Has your space room for two?
All St. Petersburg is mad and on fire!

Then away, across those infinite steppes
Held up at their points like black tents, they sing,
No Asian illness in them,
Of alabaster work above.

The Paxtons

What dreams are by overcast and autumn
Eyes seen, heard from an ethereal speech
Like wind chimes or oil that falls naked,
Or written as the trees would be letters?
It's here the Paxtons walk the killing wood.
Two Paxton men with Paxton wives make good
By a great hooded hound—what ill intent
Have such a blackest party with the house
Of God? None! For all airs are just a flight
Of chickadees from morning bath-stones,
And just as quickly the nightmare-nothing
Thought itself thought-out throughout the morning.

But what is left—beginnings
As endless children come,
Abandoned to the forest floor
And ouroboric thumb.

Pratzen Heights

The last summer lays its twilight softly
O'er our three children's sexes on the hill—
Her legs growing too long to be much more.
Were we really in that grassy vanguard
Once? From our own Pratzen Heights and same sky,
A shuttle-sight races the background by
The unbearable view for what were years
Measured and so must move past measurement—
Forgetting of the question, asking out
To whom if we would be shows to the stone?

My celebration, silent in still frame—
The wet wild tamed and wedding
Fixtures set with simple white,
Deep in the garden green, and golden rings—
Little things signifying
Love but beset by the rite—
Those in the rows of the world will have me!

And e'er I take it back again,
For though the day is for our lives,
I give my dreams to them—
Child-choirs sempiternal and fixed
As pale and winding draperies
Suffering the chancel—

Beyond, a hidden daughter
By now within her nines—
Held tight against her little chest,
Her elephant in lines.

American plastic

The sounds of summer tides accompany
Projection through American plastic—
Sunshine staining orange ice,
While air-conditioned bassinets behind
Dark blinds are hidden by teenage mothers
Against the bright flyovers—
Sounds of freedom for the star citizen—
He will fall on knees before his fathers,
Their imperial twilight
Setting parallax to the far skyline
And nearer cairns of day's Virginia dunes
Now devoid of young lovers
But pairwise prints, giving up their people
To the nightly civilian world—what man
Keeps vigilant at his post?

"Requesting authority to order,
Sir!" There is no one on the telephones,
In all the lobbies—across the rifting
Of stark shipping space, little lights marking
Precarious passage beyond the beach.
Pray some enemy hides there in the waves.

Breslau's crowds

The lamp set out by mother—
No dimness there—instead,
That furtive place of what is not
Will sit upon the bed.

End—the swells of overture ring right,
And Breslau's crowds cheer for their royalty
But for a second—afterward to yards,
A patchwork-earth to floor the summer day
Unseen in what a maze of vinyl heights,
For all colored chalk is left strewn about,
Hieroglyphics silently abandoned
For swimming pools washing words with the act—
Mandalic man dances on dark highways
Until, above all living things, some kind
Of diamond, the Emperion steps forth
And back—explodes the afternoon in gasp
A childhood to live, the score, the switch,

And fades away the terror
As through the flooring glow
The lights and loving whispers from
The kitchen down below.

Avatar

Sudden avatar, real-rendered
With a serious order, started—
I'm looking for the dolman.
One sunless lawn, self-illuminated,
Its autogamous winds, and treeless,
Day's moon almost falling in its largeness—
Full look, no movement through the faces.
Alone, barren of any mnemic trace,
I can count the polygons—
But as I believe, still my feet feel
Their bare delight upon the grass.

Between massive times
I would occasionally find
Such a small spot, black with bits of charcoal,
And some indefinite print—
If measured and found perfect,
I might have left a message in the ash,
But my finger can't make the lines.
Still, what would I say?

Hermaphroditic, stillborn me and you,
Both our body and sepulcher, we knew
Whole worlds in miniature—
Now I see in your eyes all banners raised—
Double rath—where is the center of two?
One the druid, one the frail,

And none called orphan
Watches the raindrop-whale
Across the highway window—
It sees shuddering, suffering,
To white noise—obverse, they say music.

New *Hamamelis*

Mary brings a history,
Proven either the straightaway
Or that terrible touching point—
Like propellant, thrown rock to rocket ship,
And for it summer lips in blood will crack—
Her darling boys with eyes wracked strip
Her down, daughterless, on new earths,
Plows wreak what may, birthing more.

Such musings keep our time,
The final camp set most above—trembling
Power lines, their gravity overhead
Neither a remnant nor necessity,
Still taken to be tread for what there is—
The valley-forth has God as the granite
To back once again with devilish seeds—
This is the edge to him, the vale-being
Feeling to follow where his people were.
Yet traces of a burning catch man's eye,
And all the flies are blind in their new worlds
Like babes—*to sleep, to sleep.*

When nature takes on night to hide her moths,
Sense becoming perfume and limbs are had
To be powdered, just a touch would drop deep
To the blue grass—*love.* So spell-step, dreamer!
Into the carnal gale with flushing life
As its particulates—columns in day
Were ash, now line the darkest galleries!

The wreckage of morning—
Gray seas, their fern-flowing
And swells of thunderheads
Hear singing, a northeastern voice—
Waste me! Wind-wasted energy!
Our new *Hamamelis* looks down
The cloudy batteries—soon sounds
Of noonish raindrops start the fall,
Exploding liquid day
In her, crying, loving—
The same, her mossy clutch.

Nature at her table

This morning, pregnant with midday, unseen
Frost from spring airs never known has become
To the disregarding leaves more green light—
A clear-clad bride for her water-wedding
Wonders how he used to be—his body,
Once a golden thing with its greater wheels
Like the planetary houses moving
Through the void volume of a real girl's mouth
Unmoving now, all else open face looks,
But in his eyesight was cinder—she knew
Ruin—tears and chyle, a belly between—
They would be guilty—the horrent child knows:

Nature at her table,
Thin arms touch on white cloth,
The metal finery
Around wrists and the neck,
Perfume of rain-washed stone,
Strings to skin—blue or blonde,
Cups of fornication
Raised alone in the bath,
Tile turned red, blood-filling,
The unlike lamb beside,
She is a grave—no earth
In it, and his father.

And when at last
The dimmer luminaries consider
Our distant world in their own arrangement
And assume her, that she stands, full moon-posed,
The referent—one hand resting upon
The mature animal in four colors,
The other of liquid silver extends
To paradise.

Empty church

The whole world to their backs, no Dibble House,
Dreary eyes face their the grasses dying,
Drinking stygian rains, brown and drying,
To the focal point—mother's empty church.
He stands, suited, beside his newest bride
Bruised, a little bit of blood on her dress,
And silent since her diary was left
By box and bedside innumerable—
Strokes of beauty, strokes of wife once written,
He now rewrites man and woman equal
As you can imagine—rows of blackthorn
Crawl o'er the borough, apple here and there
When the roebuck passes in memory.

September is never so dark
To a child, still full with motion,
Unabandoned yet to its life—
Is there fire in it? That burning
Calendar in the kitchen moves
Unopposed through the festal year
For years and years until their tears
And everyone are gone,
And it is here.

Part II:
In this natural space

Those fierce macaws

It rotates through its turns again,
This iterative great machine—
And oh! Behold a fractal one!
Its burning structures dissipate
In trailing tracers—irises,
White quartzy fingers, spiral-stars,
And how bright spark those fierce macaws!

Mortal light

From all illumed and sourceless fell the sun—
Now a very mortal light to but scan,
But why? Who had in mind the afternoon?
Level, space brackish with the day looks on
Their verdant parks—such sport, an oblation—
Honest play would hark the flying saucer,
Though made malleable by man so tamed
And thrown about the grasses as a toy—
Its lens, the moony witness of their lives—
It asks: "You think these summer lawns won't end?"

October fog

October fog again to hide
The trees by bloody autumn dyed
Upon, still green, near frosted,
And sunrise lit, the grass
To hold as well the smoking tents—
The gaining of the glass

Collecting all the red man's days
To lay them down before the blaze.
Yet as for now just sleeping,
Eyes gone to see the good
As mantids in the dream like leaves
Upon another wood

That stands so as to touch its boughs!
But passions from the slumber rouse!
And all again are burning,
Illuming in the black
That from the bottom of the clock
The ash is falling back.

A hidden green

In triple face the goddess gives
But a gift of gravity,
There to run beneath boughs
Inside a hidden green,
A verdant hearth, a home—
The wet babe, mute before the storm—
Its glassy worlds in droplets
Drum their limitless leaves:
"I love you with the soil.
I kiss you with the ground."

Her great horns lower for winds off Titan,
The firmamental beast, and cloudy kings
Earth-eyed and they grip their towering steel.
But all mothering brings boldness in time,
And grown sons give a requisite to sport—
So they steal upon the bright parks, water
In exhibition, for playing between
Showers and pleasure in the petrichor.

Extended blue

The air is thin, more aromatic earth,
And the world's daughter comes across,
Larger, climatic, and all life—
She throws me through the flowerheads
By which, their colors, I can see
The ordinary ease of everyday.

Breathe easy, your sacred heart,
Though attention in the pretense of the face
Would have you a stitching scene,
Up and extended blue, blush pieces in pink,
A great halcyon away,

That far-back field is never heard
By endless winter-greeted bird,
As from the dry and frosted cage
Released upon the human stage,
The chickadee is blind! Is raw!
Too much of bloody science saw!

Black to the concrete, dying wings—
For snow-white perches, quiet sings.

Blackened boughs

High blackened boughs branch through the clay,
But no breeze flits their fungal leaves,
While unseen roots stretch deep in day—
Down! Down to drink dark veins of light—
So stands the tree the worm perceives
As he picks fruited ammonite.

Ring-cupped oak

In summer's heat, upon a verdant hill,
A ring-cupped oak stands live in southern light,
And on its foot, inching his tiny will,
The greenest little caterpillar slight.
He turns his head up to the blue and sees
Long hopeful fingers spread free o'er the sky—
Unbounded choices silhouetting breeze!
So up he crawls his chosen path on high.
His eagerness strikes down the wooden parts,
Unaware of their forking iron chains.
Yet steady march finds northern leaves' red hearts,
Which fall—last, at cold chosen tip he gains
Oak's majesty collapsed into a line!
But 'neath gray clouds, alas! Acorn divine!

Throbbing mayapple

Bold youth do year and year again
Drink their springtime gin to excess.
Up! Up! The throbbing mayapple
Stands turgid in the rainy crowd
With each its parasol insured:
"Let more! And oh! How we will dance
The dripping damp of all the wood
In ever-morning-chasing-chime!"
But come the orgy's noontime sun,
Alien dust of neon rust
Does grace the lovely bodies' lust
Now crippled, lying dead among
The quiet mat of summer leaves—
A thousand ravaged boys and girls,
Above which watch the tragedy
Again the weeping oaky age.

Little figures

I used to see little figures—
Evidence of their slight things,
Prints and leaves moved about—
Actor! Actor! How they'd applaud,
Call me angel, scream my name
In the backyards, and hold
The world steady to their living
Tracers—all fluorescence in
And out of sight, but say
Nothing to my parents—pick up
Stones turned wine-colored and set
Them in my crown, for by
Most riotous declarations
They gave me supreme title
O'er everything, a child.

Today I occasionally unearth
Seashells on the mountaintop and ponder—
Wet—what superior waters?
Ears plugged like a pearl diver, it rushes
And the long-form legs of the triple crane
Breach into this thin world below—
I feel voices flit past the submerged mind
As children laugh and tell secret nonsense,
But I cannot really hear them.
Yet I will recall from bits of that speech,
Words beyond the vestigial body,
That I was master all along.

The vivid procession

Above the world and ours as well,
They serpentine the essential
As if the air became the seas—
The azure sinks down to immerse
Each sight up to their immense forms
In ancient congers—slow strokes, both
Unaware of massive motion,
Dim purpose for all their brilliance,
And let fall simple lettering—
Lights to be lamped across cities,
Flashing brief lives, phosphenes to each
On their own northward piazza,
Part of the vivid procession,
E'er to sustain, yet if complete
Would leave glazen earth—purest sheet.

Thoughts at large

Safe in some cirque
To think those thoughts at large,
Evergreen and blue-lit lowly,
Inebriating satellite, white wine
Moon, but man is speechless—
Words on the fingers, in the trees—
A midnight pool darts with silver fishes,
And on bare flesh, red studded seat,
A fairy titters with her flaming fruit—
Future-food, reposed in the molecules.

By their conversation turned
Around, the bookish boy sees
Her in her brushstrokes, and she,
Entertained in a big way,
Lets herself to be taken
Back to his eigengrau room—
All sex in the head, they say.

Yet in the college morning,
The front house cut with light,
Just human girls with half their clothes
And happy from the night.

To the little chickadee

To the little chickadee,
Here a plastic place to nest,
For the verdant trees are felled—
No mind that the poor child-fox
Has no wings to fly away.
Still do man and songbird part
Fondly, though he knows his sin?
She's gone until she perches,
Set in a ring of silver
With her form of colored glass
Pink, fluttering communion
Before pews of skeletons,
Who for a brief hymn witnessed
The glory—*breath*—of—*breath*—*chirp chirp*!

Seabright

"My love, I'll have the burden,
And you can take the way—
For me, the dread Atlantic sounds—
For you, Pacific day!"

Boy on boy that eternal Magellan
Across the endless over-earth and edge
In the pale light of his moony harbor
Faces, each with the double decision
At his two-fold bridge to offer up what
For his swimming people? The shale-shadow
Of oceans—human, those very waters.

"Flow fair, Seabright—sunburst and eight bells aft!
The due deed not yet done, but who can say?"

The juniper

Their concrete is clean—
All movement to time, on time—
Then why to my ways,
Lamplight streaking, streaming
In the paradisiacal city,
I see I don't belong?
The streets are empty
To me—I'm invisible,
Foreigner—goodbye.

A wish to away to the juniper—
Glowing gray about some high neighborhood night,
Empty and naked in the open space,
The boreal tinctures pour across my eyes
Like a deep thousand kinglets in their ivy—
I feel the beauty and abandonment

At the terminal—
My fingers are seizing—
I see them and smile,
Knowing why a wife is gone—
Swiss accounts, empty—
Left for some dancing thing—
Nothing, but plenty.

A Mid-Atlantic Easter

A Mid-Atlantic Easter—
The birds hop in a happy procession
Through the chapel-halls of seed—
If one keeps them in their bushes,
Technicolor chickadees,
The robin is singing a mother's song,
And perches ring as the bells.

Yet come the end of the sunny season
The pores of the earth pull beneath the sands,
Space and its Jovian drones returning,
Their emergence in some cosmic time forth
To drive all else to passion once again—
And in the dimming of the summer flash,
If evaded the royal walk, what throes
Flare their last great structures on the flatness—
Brightest latticework of the world away.

Racing our fairgrounds on stilted costumes,
Their brilliant flags, each a dragon-flourish,
So golden earth is raised for barefoot steps
Blazing up to starships' symphonic airs—
Dazed spring grains to sun flares.

Ruby-throated hummingbird

There is but one flitting thing,
An iridescence
In boundless jeweled points each giving
Its own far facet a structure, sense
To the opalescent forms—
The small finery
Of its machinations moves and storms,
Thundering in silver enginery
He is unable to hold,
Flicking, flickering, and fussing
Only its consequences
Across his view, like a baby
Sees past its hanging mobile
The ruby-throated hummingbird
Roaring through the nursery
And out before its name is said.

The chemical estate

Wide fountains with their amaranthine whorls—
This, the chemical estate,
By generation
Made and left for its white-robed children—
Spirits within, without.

Long birds, all mechanical in their ways,
Watch o'er the gardens and its pale creatures—
Just knees and ankles they follow
The great gold aurochs maundering
Past the mazes of hazels
And stone-salmon in their Penrose pools,
The sea stars on the paths.

Vermillion comes to their whispering cheeks
When little rumors of some cutting room
Pass between them—there they say, forms
And the entelechy of things
As they are for themselves known—
Bronze half-men still in the glass foyers,
Silent on the subject.

No sulfur in their stares, utter and out
The windows to the moisture
In the morning dew—
That living blight upon the orchards
And sun's shadow conceived.

How quiet

How quiet lies the universe—
The scenes of lighted rain,
Their sights gray out, a fading sound
From afternoons of pain.

But what exactly is it of?
These window-summer storms,
They seem so clear—their falls define
The definite of forms

Out what must be the infinite
That must be known to be—
It rings aloud for just itself
Itself itself to see.

Southern seas

With white wood still on the Arctic waters,
Stellar distances, for off his lashes
Roll the galaxies, the monkey-mirror
And the stars watch the last animation
Of a man cry: "I ask for the judges!"
Past the cold extent and that unconscious
Personality's infolding, eyesight
Outpouring, the southern seas are endless!
It's here all drifting things must come naked—
The black winds keep warm, their opaline lamps
Like thunderclouds—the luminescent verve
Laps its billions on countless shallow strands—
Through such infinite arrangement he sleeps
With each, a different lover, but a night.

Origin

Young boy, happy only on the front,
His purpose quietly purls beneath
The docks, murmurings of sleepy murder—
A child, his moving humors whirl,
And all men grow dark, but Shade or Shadow?

Titanic mills, clean in their white future,
Rise rank and sail on summer hills
As green and blue breezes, upstate somewhere—
Iridule for the low-lake heron
And origin for the new man's life.

Part III:
What we may carry

The little man

The little man, he sees it so
On just one ball of many, though
So far away in still array—
But how dark synchronicity
Moves unobserved and unaware
Of him as he of it cannot but dream—
And yet in pride he still declares
To know from only how it seems.

Come rave!

Come rave! Into the garden!
The gala lights are low—
The rhythm runs through all the girls,
Their eyebrights' double glow.

For what comes moving tonight, witch?
Star or laser-light switch—ground and sound pitch.

From whose eyes will you see the eschaton?
As just some Moorish Cide, e'er the witness,
Writes what across the city-rails climbing?
Lit up by earth-embers, the fields finished
At the end and the scattering of ships

From newly sighted distance,
A horror dark and drawn
Strokes high about its mimicking
Their human, skyline, gone.

The sorry boy from Watertown

The sorry boy from Watertown
Has his gaze parsed upon the scene,
A land from some Americana life—
To the left, a pretty saintess,
And out of Vietnam they come,
Motherless children, taken to be taught—
To the right, like looming airships,
Silent clouds o'er the field houses
Holding out and such little lives as his.

How strange that postwar life as a lake-edge
Has his wishing now standing springtime moss—
What light seashell hands touch only the bed—
Her offspring back to their dark recesses,
Clean-swept from stately highway shores,
The steam of noodles in their bowls
As though a grand aquarium
Flowing alive in Saigon streets.

On the rim

Make good on adolescence—
In blonde and blue, a candy blue,
Freely given will take her to morning.
Yet there a head half-pillowed
E'er greets the memorial sun
To the daily killing of the deep guard
And all time set from the deed.
So new lovers duly punished
On the racks of the actual, they ask
For the mundane or the fae?
Always the struggle on the rim—
Try at the muses, their margins, and die.

The bathroom

I used to talk to the bathroom fixtures,
Deliberating decision with them,
Before to be dead in the far showers
Behind their steel doors—colored for children?
Or here, where what the reader imagines
At the oars of some sparkling world's waters—
The fish fill the boats on their own accord,
And from that sphere of sky fall rainbow rains
Upward as well, until all grounds are wet
With the Lethe—pumped back to the washrooms
By way of diamond pipes we lay ourselves.

Twilit town

Their lives were all of white—no wolven red
Yet stops the poor necessity of boys
To leave the crags for warmer waterways—
A world of bryophyte long by the square
And gate, a twilit town—his line of girls.
Corridors. Corridors. How's it rendered?
The whole scene set with charges, laced with light,
And new earth folded up. Row young Tolstoy!
No North American night for great men!

"My color is royal.
My body is big.
Feel at the metabolism and see it so!"

Byways Bennett and balding hills
Back to his argent people
As effigies of sulfur-stone,
Lifeless breeding, water-bleeding,
And mutually alone.

Annalight

The grand ascent—the gradient!
All captains to the radiant!
Brass put upon the astral slopes—
A father's odds for his far babe.
What to tell the philosophical son
To be? Was he once sated with the man
And Thomas-touching in the upper rooms?
"That nothing coalesces into hands…"

But leave off this gastrulation—
Begging boys will beg for you:
"Sing the tale of Annalight! Tell it true!"

So something of a fairy,
Self-same with the virgin vale.
Let saunter down a giant—
The happiness of lovers?
Her fluid tastes like gasoline!
His promise-lips are lies!
Its burning diamonds, ashen earth
Is black by valley skies.

As such stories go on, man weeps
At the phantasmagoria,
Wide-eyed, enraptured with his dad.
The charade is such a burden,
Yet the thing of sole importance.

Poses as a girl

Does the scientist dare to take the bat,
The larger of the two, in hands assured
And split the skull that poses as a girl?
To break the little legs that run through fields
Where she picks daisies in a smiling farce?
For is it of his duty just to prove
That when there twists his heart within his chest,
The pressure of the heat across the gaze,
It is just as the daughter's but a doll?
So his blow too won't swing but only fall.

Which ward?

E'er first cries for authority—which ward?
Babes being washed with ink, black christening
And the self-flourish of a signature—
Certificates of living—for these words
Lifelong lovers thrust in vital panic,
Working the cascades and crystal bowers—
Red hedges trimmed of flesh and bloody swans,
Pulled by perspective, float by lesser lamps—
There the blur of animality comes
As locked rooms, harlequin, aureolin,
Celeste, and a single mosaic man—
Silhouette, no sight in isolation,
But that half-hating smile turned all inward
To where some hospital or another
Minds the imaginal automata.

Another day of carnival

Another day of carnival
With chalky whites and bloody meat,
About which acid color-sweet
In glassy holds, it roars! It rings!
A prompt by bird on broken wings
Says sunburn and the itching bite,
But faint beside revolver's light!

Yet children must be wary of evening
When the gas goes out—a carnality
Comes skulking between Midwest and midway:
"Offer here! Offer here! Run off your homes!"
And in the dark, the sensation recurs
At once to be in many little lives.

Come fair anew! The old in ash
Is blown away as piled trash—
But short a generation,
Dear parents—far away!
It's just another carnival.
It's just another day.

Documented

Trial 4-26-573

"How sphexish are their passions!
Another comes to be
So hopeful for her wedding day—
Begin 573."

Metal likewise naked wakes the woman—
Each breath, a shudder that plays forever
In such a sealed place, dissipated yet
E'er implicit—where before, a promise?
From fetal embrace and eyed embrasure
Violent with a hope all direness draws,
She pulls along the maze, from vent to vent—
The blow of her lover! But mixed among
Many more men! So swelled and starved, she casts
To a guessed pipe, and documented, dies.

"Well now, do you think that was a success?"
"I don't know. What are we even doing?"

A sunlit moment

The sward as though a city
Ventures forth its bare boy,
But ordered in his articles—
Other beings! Back again!
On guard against the sounds
Now, he finds flight by knowing sleep—
Feel at the length of deep time
Not quite apprehended,
But remembered unbearably
Born—the simian sunsets
Uncounted and alone.
Until here, past all enemies
Lies his sleek ship at the line—
With power and with light,
Unto the fast ways from the wood
Away into a future!

Wild eyes, starred upon their grassy passage,
Flash on the roadside, and the great whirring
Of the shuttle gives their form a dark deer
For a sunlit moment set in escape.

As do their dreamers

Take care, for civilizations in head
Run like clocks as do their dreamers—
And whether the asters grow mountainous
Or embers pull the flicker-forms
Of young girls to see the lady in each,
The boys but fast adumbrations—
The fish-face in the fire is shuddering,
And in its orb a human babe

Is ripped into its being
And blasted to the floor!
Here man must take his keeper's role
Against their begging more.

In death or a woman

In death or a woman I find myself
Seeing with a newfound violet view
As though saddled on sight of some great bird
Racing from out the lofty charnel house,
The empty space of a huge hollow world,
And always into that last Eresos—
Its luxurious walks, sea-warm midnight,
With like eyes amethyst and alien
Watching on *Solanum* stalks the dark surge
Of that other ouzo-tide to swallow
All the laughter, low lights, and terraces—
In my spine there moves a matrix of rooms,
No box unbound by her form so eigen
And essentially outbreeding her sons.

Thus, my terminal man becomes became—
Just a brief cry, recurring, maternal,
In eternal feminine flame.

Old professor

Old professor, his sharp breathing
At when the chest begins to push,
Puts forward all his scholarship—
But their minds are disassembling,
Science slipping, words fall away
With pen and paper to the floor,
And the lapwing, no longer still
In her type specimen, leaves him
Meaningless.

He staggers out onto the day,
Long life between unlit lampposts—
The young bodies, they start to swirl
In their own small autumns like leaves,
And the last light comes on singly
In flash, from brilliance, a student—
His ashen wife burning again
Before everything acted out
Becomes fire.

Our bloodlines lost,
Pumped out of the earth by pipes
Until no one is anyone
Anymore—the field lilies
Floating in the oil and dead fish
Consider us.

Silver cay

The penultimate moment—
A simple image of periwinkles,
The cannonade to my initials,
None of greater men.
This is the measured instance
Before, black-robed, my life-crowned king is back
Taken throughout the blanket-blackness
To that silver cay
Revolving, like coincidence,
Its Boolean footprints still in the sand.
There's no man here to ask the dust and flies
Of my living, with dark children running
Through the buildings, time in their eyes seeing
Darker men. Can you speak of it truly
As itself past comparison?
Yet in this awesome trembling,
Gloriously, an answer to myself
Raises up its parti-colored face
Above all events
And groans out loud such a low
Frequency as that ten billion people
In their great crawling machines across
A barren planet.

Pipe and box

Those brave machines of Switzerland!
To climb their colored cranes
And spend the days a starving man
Who, pulled among the trains,

Does drown in deep a foggy sea—
Gray belfries as the boats
Loom tall, forlorn about the clouds
That settle on the coats,

That settle on the drunken dogs
And o'er the chiming clocks—
Their ringing times each moment's end
And march of pipe and box.

Concrescence

Remembering remnants of spring—what was
Eye-uttered from that Appalachia?
Just passing in and out of worlds, I see
One Golconda, likewise through me,
My children made of metal, light, or more?
And ending all permutations of school,
Thorny burnets like the gravestones—
Girls breathing give structure on the passing
Breath, bare feet feel the circumstantial floors,
And sight, the concrescence of iris-dice.

So let alone a look alight—
Such things have never been before
And e'er not to reconvene—
Infinity is clean.

Starship girl

Oy! Starship girl! So far away!
How fares that other sky?
The ground beneath those altered suns?
The clouds o'er which you fly?

For here the grass is brightly green,
The firmament is blue,
The Sunday train rolls on its tracks
Beneath the mountains' view,

And I look up to see your life
Reflected in the guess—
You're so much more than I could be,
And I am so much less.

The young poet

I was made image of the diamond mind—
One man before that adamantine wall
Of words forever in all directions
So conceives himself in congregation—

Endless rows of faceless forms
As they extend to have him
Moan out, muted in the dark—
This is a frenzy of speech.
Imposter, who writes the lists?
The young poet repossessed
And made sick for his efforts

Is by woman judged, alike delivered,
And that girl Gina, small and smoking, comes
With woad-stained skin and alphabetic bag
Kept close: "Will you kiss me for your letters?"

"But oh, my dear! I'm married!
A Christian, so I stand
In sight of God, I ask instead
If I could kiss your hand."

Part IV:
Or whom we love

I call you mistress, Lesvos

I call you mistress, Lesvos—
Your kisses with sirocco-lips
Command a boy to blue and breasts
Of tiny shells as polished bells and stone—
Mosaic tunes of afternoons in tones.
The breath in clear Aegean
Sighs entire days of summer—
You give your fertile ground, but there
Solanum seed the earth to bleed by right—
The waves in debt, young love to sweat the bight.

So to work upon your ovules
In mirage of the Turkish hills,
Watching with purple irises
Through ouzo-glass or microscopes?
But what kind of man would take her?
This being, clean, empiriant,
With one, just water, by his veins—
Holding up no category
Of slighter men, their weight in worlds,
Seeing the suns of all vision,
Such minute lives—he becomes them.

Eyesight is burning, bare feet are aflame,
And the whole Grecian world comes in clear fire.

Upon the Monmouth

What love is of hallucinated kind?
How real that she should e'en leave her footprints,
Their insidious steps, in his wife's world.
So *shake, shake, shake*—narrows that sphexish sight.
But *step, step, step*—she kneels at the bedside!

So make a choice! The affair
Endlessly unfolding its saffron fields—
How many boys to blossom?
How many girls bloom upon the Monmouth,
Body-begging the moments?
Yet castrated, the generations wail—
Their sex as spice spun to gold—
The cosmic parent sets the leas aflame:
"Better burning than being!"

Inflection

Zoe or Zoz—
From pattern to the process
Thoughts tiptoe, which one ought not to trace—
The holly blue on flowers
Drinks full of the sun's implicit form,
But touch its cosmic deed—death!
So snap back to which pretty girl in bloom?
What she indeed, dear Leopold,
Dances a lovely distraction upon
The dyad's diverging wake?
No lines may e'er hold their parallel,
And a prepared heart welcomes
The inflection—sick on the sidewalks,
Steps to a Circean house,
But English.

The west fields

The night performs its romance
To the walls from wild winds with lights
Like Greek houses, civic grace—
Highest windows face the west fields
As vestals to life lit low
And plucked beside its festivals.

The deep city is moving, a flower—
By petal-places the cottontail girls
Peak upon parties with their river-eyes
Glowing, faces swimming into others—
And man, profiteer, his small initial
To reconstruct the body—all curtains!
Her features like fire to the blue theater!

Leave the hearts of young daughters,
Light for a shuffle, to a bright breakfast

Alone—

The heat comes o'er the houses—
The flies will fill the days—
No shadows from the evening forms—
Their bellies feel the blaze.

Two things

On a young engagement—
Twice boys, lovers, past raping form,
But by our five-fold bond unbound to be,
Find fantasy with what we both were not
When we would doubly peer
Into that portal of solarium—
The freshness of a washroom tides and keeps
On tile what should rot—crystal crowds,
The baths, and sunlit beds.

Left, late in life, the fawn shades let
Afternoon in softly alike
To her body in the clean room.
How expensive was this bedding?
I see she has her finger bare
Today, but she does not, eyes closed,
Rapid to my fancy—cold hands
Feel her and the microstructures
Of the fabrics coming larger
Frightfully in sudden quickness!
A shudder and memory fades.
All burned, the glass pipe has fallen
Away—breathing now becomes deep—
Her chest, it starts to hum—she moans
Lowly, and I imagine what
Unknown man, ephemeral life,
His ceaseless diction, is to her.

Upon these two things I think
Run through to three,
And one, the third, is happy—
Is counted me.

Beauty in blue and beauty in white

Beauty in blue and beauty in white—bright
Miss, you like the tinsel on the wild pines.
But there, hidden in the load, you will see
The masses of darker daughters come on
Ashen, higher, black mascara-eyes wide,
Dancing, sex becoming, bodies humming
To have your children, and men will let them.
He takes you, your lines of silver, gold drops,
To the trees, leaving—how you hate him so.

But to his mind her structures are raised up
Around every object—vision flicking
Forever all around—a flower girl
In rings of iteration, hand in hand,
Skips and singing—appalling, her spinning,
Before spring bears him a child in the reed.

Boardwalk dreams

Kentucky beasts so bridled take the tracks,
But then their forms as children in the yard—
A budding shows in gym-time uniforms,
Full legs fenced for an appropriate pair—
Such schools frame the boardwalk dreams and summer

For which the world will leave behind
Boys with the grounds and their coteries,
To see in steadfast days a return
Of the girls from sad necessity,
To stay and take unto the heels again.

To that goodbye at fire-sky
Where west another life would lie—
But here, Atlantic duty—
E'er student or a steed,
Concrescence at the ringing gun
And beauty of the breed.

Dublin asks

Nameful, she in many,
There crowned of June aflame,
Finds living in the circus or city?
And Dublin asks if she can dance
Or duet with the lights?

For liquid eyes, this fleeting lilt,
Her man against the men
Must bear that primate's fear
And e'er act, lest they take her as a doll
To lie upon communal beds,
Her form for what it's worth.
Yet if won, there his wood,
Would a husband be a different lover?

A passion for morasses!
The cutting reeds across
Her body to the toady beat—
Her tears to fuck the moss!

But not until it happens!
And what if she will yield?
Indeed, her sought surrendering
Lets power too to wield!

So how must all end, we'll to chance defer—
The gunshots rang from out them, him, or her?

A boy named Holly

With newest ways a boy named Holly comes
On faster for his harvest bride
By eighty-one and northward.

Lonely silo silhouettes disappear
As space comes down to touch the roads
And just beginning blazes on the wood
Are quickened out by the wind.
Then all night comes with single violin
Keeping, as clean leather and low controls
Rush him through the valleys and sleeping lakes
Like beasts, and the trees too become monstrous
In the headlights, roaring at second suns—
Purple alders in the dark
With heaviest eyes, driving to the dream,
The same as that synteresis
Moves him through his yearly rings, but golden.

There she poses, white in her wedding dress,
With just a smile to the query
If there is time to change things.

The sunlit lord

Way in those longest fields,
Whether with rank or wildflower,
Otherwise empty in the hard morning,
Leaving the sunlit lord
Up with his great antlers alone
In yards, treelines—there our memories
Of nobility play
As young boys, each being the last
In his line of kings waiting to be let
Through into the writ-world—
But he with bottle-broken hip
Staggers as any man through that river
In his own bed, unknown
With its new drink—honey and salt—
All stones holeless and maidens run about.

Dress her up in the small dress—
Give lipstick—say catalyst
Softly with her tongue—photos
For everyone—daughterless.

That awful cutter

He is risen—
That awful cutter,
His paring knife, to smile,
Nature's model on his arm,
Watches the lukewarm-blooded man.

In his working room like a chest
There keeps all kinds of bright birds
In cages of golden wire,
Lenses and little metals
Propped on the rich cherrywood,
And dark pastels—noonish glow
Of his green taxonomy
Just outside the windowpanes
Floating into oiled corners,
Quiet equal of his bijoux.

How they laugh at him—his woman,
Held a tiny Persian dancer
In her glass for exhibition
And the comment of other men.

"Cut her free? She would be
The only pale lady
Of society
Then, laying much more than
Image—blood, phantasmal
Still to him alone."

Double her

Father, see your son upright—
His pretty wife dressed in white,
Her flowers in the dropout dust,
Alternatively, and dancing
In the footage, imagining you
Baregolden, bloodline kind of beauty—
But binary—black hills by a sky-fire
Are justly windowed to witness empire
Iterate men, room on room glowing
Like blue-lit faces feigning living—
Love, it is the saddest story—
That they would feel across the screen,
Their bodies razed, wasted stand
Just usernames—sex in hand.

Yes, double her to music,
By images to breed,
Untouchable in registers
For all their human seed.

Lilith

He has them row beneath the sun
But still upon the land
On sleek machines of stainless steel
And plastic's curvature.
Their yearning slakes the shrubbery—
Their moans feed all the grove—
Yet such girls are always abandoned,
For there's tinsel in the knotted hair
Of Lilith. "You're beautiful and mad."

She talks unto the pavement
And whispers to the walls
While all the waking world's about—
A sill of silent dolls.

Clementine Quixotestein

With lissome tones, though by the summer breached,
Her winter bastions proud in ruin, reached—

Dear Clementine Quixotestein
Chews on her seven syllables,
A child dressed in fields—the corset
With the buttercups, the partlet
With wings of swallowtails in waltz
Among a hall of cricket strings,
And gems of roadside chicory
Set in a circlet of pollen—
So authored, sees her world anew:
"A mystery! A miracle!"
And finding such joy lyrical,

Yet asks about her mother
And of the life they feign:
"A home for such an alien?
Siberia or Spain?"

"Sleep until the driveway—in love I sign
To you, my Clementine Quixotestein."

Abomination

It's made of reel and ribbon—
An eeriness to glow
A likeness in the baby's eyes—
A speechlessness to know

No more in the host, pairless at the last—
Indeed, what of rights engender
Out of how many little lizard-lives,
Bush after bush is burning, man?
But let millennium prove the matter!
The old world will leave him broken—
Black Madonna with gold lilies pushing,
Being time's whorls, and receptive
To the self-same seed—his constitutions
To give alike to other girls
True-breeding and govern their fertile grounds.

They cry:
"Oh, please don't kill my children!
For what then would I be?
Abomination!"

And always back, the marram-path—
Ahead the world and all its wrath!

Cassidy!

Cassidy! Cassidy! Come to the rood,
Bridal force, with the old priest on your sword.

Your maids have all gone to the druids' day—
Erect figures, weeping for their antlers—
To step in dress, in flower, their waters
From basins made of silver stone, and set
Fawning spring its virgin gifts free-given.
Your man with his machine makes through winter—
Its blackness parted and its cold cut past
The old couples held out in their houses,
Sleeping for just some far recollection
Lost in the low-beating blood of their bed.

So three and three go by the beach—
Their human forms hung like crosses
In the sky's dawn or dusk-wide gray,
And what was once worlds up above
Finds in the meat of the motion
Something not quite so important—
A white witness horribly there
Now, uncreating—defacing.

A fairy girl

She's lying here, not quite a fairy girl,
With widest eyes much too off, like the shines
Of beetles or moving oils on wet streets—
Naked white on white desert, her small chest
Seen and overexposed in perfect day
When the hair is pulled up for a moment,
As is some slight wire from the nape laid bare,
Fills in a paroxysm of living.

I remember how it started—
If we were father and daughter,
It was just blood—that hot fullness
In me I would not have withheld—
But our one room without address,
A moving diorama, where
Through its lithe rotations she danced
For me, became the open earth.

Then this is the end of all intention—
I imagine in the requisite speech,
As the obverse everyman with his thorns
Now reflects, my sexless spirit staring
At its own among infinite bedforms—
Her young lips, being far from their purpose,
Softly utter out machine language-like
Doom visible on the shimmering breath:

"See my single face, no other
Two bemoaning love ungiven,
And that great inverted object
There in the idea of distance,
Tangent always to the center
Of vision, comes—our condition
Is temporary—enjoy me,
This body, supine on the sand."

Part V:
From that other world

Private Jacob

Endless washrooms—young boys in the mirrors
See their pale bodies already in rank—
They feel at their fathers, want them at war.
Private Jacob, you will hear them mourning,
Those images frame-freed and Marian,

Or little girls from Vietnam
Sing science for a greener dead—
The metals rhyme with tetrazole,
A counterpoint to lead.

On foreign earth you cry out:

"I am a soldier—my foes, immortal—
But in my spiral rifling, a portal
To hues half-mast at autumnal records
Alongside my own, manmade of all stone—
I will be hydraulic." Upright, alone,
Two children running beneath the icons' shelves,
Electrical-envisioning themselves.

A protean place

From the midnight airstrips, their little lights,
Earth floats up before my hands
A protean place—yet to travel it
And see its fullness of community
Asks why I am left in the dim mazes
Of lives and lampposts alone?
Better to be up in the tall blackness
Of the wild, no sight but that fiery lens,
And I see the force of my long people
Behind me—dynastic sight.
Or are they ahead, watching my moment
With malintent? What words are possible
By gods in their far uproarious place?
They sigh—deep moans without me—
At me? I am on the floor somewhere, dead.

City in chrome

Man, at the end and dirigible,
He shapes earth up into a line
And can follow it simply
To a city in chrome—
All its geometric avenues
Empty, with solid sounds booming
By his steering as though steel
Beneath him, around him—
Next to him, high-rise of fabric, flesh,
And sex in the sidecar, unseen
But through his recording eye—
Its storage to stories
Holding so many automatic
Autoclaves—clean dirt and plastic
In the nose—the only point
For pleasure to refer.

No more the passerine heart,
Swept up and by a spring,
Will suffer for the warm relief
That dying Augusts bring.

Arianrhod

February wastes of dead and gray ground—
Terrible voices overhead like planes
Whirring their mechanical siren-sounds,
And following beneath in marching lines
Those little unbaptized ones almost blue
In the cold barrens are shepherded north
By their white-bodied hounds, red ears alert,
Way back to some Arianrhod—watching,
Fathers standing stone on the far ridges
Without judgment, Idris' seat empty.
Only they see a land of dying suns
Littered as human forms across the ice—
Symbols with heads bowed, galactic silence,
Being held in place, self-speared, still on fire—
They wait for promises of mist to hide
The awful clarity of their burning,
Sight all alone, or the tides of a shore,
Blood red, to wash a past planet across

Community, wide crystallin,
And three times hyperborean.

The exhibit

A milky venue laid with lights
To give the dark a color
And outline o'er the wild rage—
A young power, sure as not
Just bodies in their time.

In the only eyes there sees a shooting
Again—dead figures on the theater floor
Giving look but glossy reflection back
At the looping of the pale reel—
Some screen illumed in eigengrau
Forever and then nothing!

Yet eternity, the briefest thing!
So silently the exhibit dims
Into e'er greater architecture—
And opening the low murmurings
Of mass, the morning museumgoers'
Tile-tapping and coffee-clutches give
Breath leverage for day to start anew.

Skylines in parallax

Mary and Mary! Make way!
For the third and thirtieth Sophia!
All external things purified,
Far from the fading phosphenes,
Will give up what richly barren being—
The exponential anthropoid.

Yet such a birth still feels the body-cord—
So a grand exodus up those wide ways
With abandoned skylines in parallax.
O'er the climbing ziggurats, like balloons,
Some drones by Fabergé, wheel and whisking,
Whir as jeweled shepherds about human
Flocks. The work finished—make merry in groves!
No mind the gates to slaughter them in droves—
Alone, they shiver in their registers.

Paperman

"Can you hear me, Pa?
How long have we been lying here?
Is it that we're dead, Pa?"

For what end is a false history signed,
Paperman? A causative veneer o'er
The humming thing set in its harmala
Lets a light of the maternity ward
See a life through an error in the eyes.
So this view is poured into the woodwork—
Every form becomes a masturbation,
And to time the mannequins are moving—
Mute pleas: "Breach my professionality!"
Dearest love stolen, sold in video—
Goat screams flashing on the spine—*Maa! Maa! Maa!*

"So am I you, Pa?
Just that I don't quite feel myself.
Oh! But please don't say it!"

Leopold and Lotty

In wastes of sand forever,
More spine than that it holds,
A headdress made of scimitars,
Aborted wings in fold—

Yet that only face is turned away,
And before its back lives a brief life—

A Leopold and Lotty
See no difference between them,
Exploring spring, eidetic
Leas, as children hand in hand
In feeling, no mind to touch
The form besides the leaf buds.

But all growing things come to be grown,
And the candelabra-head has turned—

A sadness is the solitary beast,
For demon-dressed, the sorry act to be
Must put array, its crinkling, still again
To the ceaselessness of the dust-filled day.

The silent hyperhound leads the scene
Forwards—turn to red seas of impulse—

And e'er expanding city
Salutes the drive ahead—
There, mechas too show vital force
Beside the girls in bed.

The Light Man

A morning in the highway seeming sets
All crafts into the afternoon,
Whirring any other coffee-casing
But for panic of the viewer—

An anxiousness imagined?
Tearing at the edges of vision,
The outer roar grows in an Eleusis—
Being too becomes labored—
A fear that e'en the trees need be braced
Lest the whole scene would open in an ease,
And peering through—the Light Man!
Assembly cracks beneath his up-step!
Colossal lips give what words as worlds out
Soundlessly in sight—he sees?

Echoes of a replaying,
And so cries: "Agency! Autonomy!"
"Would you not make love to me?"
"Oh! Let me lay the world instead—in lies!"

Set to a screen, left to run out as such,
War as if were scripted, though never touch
To its fields, takes much and gives to purpose.

A glitch

From out the crash, upon the snow,
There sits the weeping woman's throe—
But one of shock! Amazement's touch
At that the body sits as such
And sees those vivid depths of air
Where but a moment past did stare.

What lurks about periphery—
The cross upon *Cruciferae*—
A bloodless breathing nothing real,
And too its looks of malice steal
By fading thoughts—a fool for eyes
Into a view—collapsing whys.

She stalls, a glitch—did something switch?
It's dead where once in life was rich.

The holy traps

And at the end there lies nothing but fields—
Their molten stretches reach
By such distance and pitch
Far into dark plumes of the horizon.
The mental strings, clockwork ticking, and chimes—
A counterpoint to moves of metal wheels
And unbounded tracks high above the fires.
Look at the wristwatch—always that ninth hour—
Feel back to those vibrations of the glass
On the forehead, remembering no more
Ordeals of living and early morning
Lamplight marking ways through cities where she,
With what blonde braid put up to be undone,
Skips along the songlines,
Instep keeping dreamtime—
Did we make love in my delirium?

To be
In her banding hands becomes worship—
Our triple eyelight on that picture
Puts to green country a brilliant coast
As if drawn, sunshine to the essence,
Cut by ditherings of a smaller
Cabin where we in single icon
Are gold.

But instead, just one rotting frame—
Theotormon and Oothoon lit
Dimly by an emetic third.

Yet such memorized visions pass orange
Beyond the focus of a window-thought—
Long lava seas to bring again regret,
For all infinity is now beheld—
Eternal visage of the holy traps
Burning a hot reality beneath
New trains that roar forever straight ahead.

Low-hanging sun

As is the unbearable animal
To our race, bodies cast aside by man
On beds of sheet or soil, that angel-eye
Looks out briefly on the cold clicking gears—
A bottom-zero nakedness alone,
In the dark, and we've been here forever.
Step out of the stream and see the vacuum
Fluctuation come back around again—
The low-hanging sun in collapsing sight,
Walking e'er after those careful jewels—
What are your lines, Fleur? Shaking in our arms,
I'm nodding, and our creode comes deeper.

That great black glass

Just another night and I am alone
In the craft, low-light meters to the dark,
Quite comfortable on highways—that secret
Said aloud: "I just want to be happy."
Out of the small window I see my way—
Procession through the planetary halls.
And from such deep reflection, the streetlights
In their dyad, across the wet pavement
Becoming singly, give that great black glass—
Below, towering pillars of flame grow,
Those Enoch saw, passing so much distance
Every second—yet their immensities,
Impenetrable to our miniature
World, are merely mirrored in its portions.
I think that if I could slow my vessel
And step out to that water-wasted edge,
At the interface with my double, make
One last man of fire-garnet and amber.
Both our paired face looks o'er immiscible
Creation, imagining a moment
Swimming about in the golden-haired bursts
Between twin rivers—swaths of pale psyche

As a boundless stone gyre—
All whom I know in single row,
Mouths open, gasping at one another,
Eye to eye with the fish.

My accolades

To say something of my accolades?
In the end, sterile, and at the long tone,
Have I reached you, my living audience?
Or am I just some Zemblan king running
To die unwritten by another's hand?
I have passed through the animal room yet,
Without correction or calling it white,
Far moon—her dark lipstick says memory,
A fairy punctuation on the night
As above, below, for what fantasy
Reposes in the deep earth, residing
As a son in my wife—amusement's place.
Do I plot against me, fiery father?
Make my pyric parts anew from nothing?
Those are my honors. Who will salute?

What man has to give

And what has man to give upon
That rolling world in endless iteration?
Atop the e'er repeating bulwarks
He stands, though stunted, stalwart,
For by that hidden faith, rewashed
With fear or feigned as but a foolish woman,
Push forward his bitterest fingers
Against the cloudy reaches
As though his own were cast above—
To his eyes they mold their empyrean ways,
But his defiant Job smashes it
To scrape the requisite sores.
The first burn of the story fades
And just its ashy words are left to gather—
Their drifts to tell what only was once
And ask what man has to give.

"I ain't no showman, boys and girls,
But neither not the dawn—
The morning sun is everything!
And everything is gone!"

References

1. Palmer, J. 2020. "Parmenides." *The Stanford Encyclopedia of Philosophy*. Ed. E.N. Zalta.
2. Joyce, J. 2012. *Ulysses*. New York: Vintage Classics.
3. Cohen, F.S. 1929. What is a question? *The Monist* 39(3):350-364.
4. Benson, H.H. 2010. "Socratic Method." *The Cambridge companion to Socrates*. Ed. Morrison D. Cambridge: Cambridge University Press.
5. Clauberg K.W., Dubislaw W. 1923. *Systematisches wörterbuch der philosophie*. Leipzig: F. Meiner.
6. Gall M.D. 1970. The use of questions in teaching. *Review of Educational Research* 40(5):707-721.
7. Bloom B. 1956. *Taxonomy of educational objectives*. vol 1: cognitive domain. New York: McKay.
8. Overholser J.C. 1993. Elements of the Socratic method: I. systematic questioning. *Psychotherapy* 30(1):67-74.
9. Navia L. 1985. *Socrates: the man and his philosophy*. Lanham: University Press of America.
10. Seeskin K. 1987. *Dialogue and discovery: a study in Socratic method*. Albany: SUNY Press.

11. Aschner M.J. 1961. Asking questions to trigger thinking. *NEA Journal* 50:44-46.
12. Vale R.D. 2013. The value of asking questions. *Molecular Biology of the Cell* 24(6):680-682.
13. Foulk T.G. 2000. "The form and function of koan literature." *The koan: texts and contexts in Zen Buddhism.* Eds. Heine S., Wright D.S. Oxford: Oxford University Press.
14. Aitkin R. 1990. *The gateless barrier: The wu-men kuan (mumonkan).* San Francisco: North Point Press.
15. Asahina S. 1931. "Zen no kōan." *Zen, vol. 3.* Ed. Nagasaka Kaneo. Tokyo: Yūzankaku.
16. Carroll L. 1872. *Through the looking glass, and what Alice found there.* London: Macmillan.
17. Graves R. 1948. *The white goddess: a historical grammar of poetic myth.* London: Faber.
18. Graves R. 1965. *Mammon and the black goddess.* London: Cassell.
19. Huxley A. 1952. *The devils of Loudun.* London: Chatto and Windus.
20. von Goethe, J.W. 1994. *Faust, part two* (D. Luke, Trans.). Oxford: Oxford University Press.
21. Proust M. 2003. *In search of lost time. vol I: Swann's way.* New York: Modern Library.

Acknowledgments

Grateful acknowledgment is made to the editors of the following publications in which versions of these poems first appeared:
Sheila-Na-Gig Under 30, Volume 5: "Ruby-throated hummingbird"
In Parentheses, Volume 6, Issue 2: "Nature at her table"
In Parentheses, Volume 6, Issue 2: "Another day of carnival"

Title Index

A

Abomination 92
A boy named Holly 86
A fairy girl 94
A glitch 107
A hidden green 37
American plastic 24
A Mid-Atlantic Easter 48
Annalight 62
Another day of carnival 65
A protean place 99
Arianrhod 101
As do their dreamers 68
A sunlit moment 67
Avatar 26

B

Beauty in blue and beauty in white 83
Blackened boughs 39
Boardwalk dreams 84
Breslau's crowds 25

C

Cassidy! 93
City in chrome 100
Clementine Quixotestein 91
Come rave! 57
Concrescence 73

D

Documented 66
Double her 89
Dublin asks 85

E

Empty church 32
Extended blue 38

F

Father Hux 19

G

Good morning fairgrounds! 16

H

How quiet 51

I

I call you mistress, Lesvos 78
In death or a woman 69
Inflection 80

L

Leopold and Lotty 105
Lilith 90
Little figures 42
Low-hanging sun 110

M
Mortal light 35
My accolades 112
My credentials 17

N
Nature at her table 30
New *Hamamelis* 28

O
October fog 36
Old professor 70
On the rim 59
Open window 20
Origin 53

P
Paperman 104
Pipe and box 72
Polenka 21
Poses as a girl 63
Pratzen Heights 23
Private Jacob 98

R
Ring-cupped oak 40
Ruby-throated hummingbird 49

S
Seabright 46
Silver cay 71
Skylines in parallax 103
Southern seas 52
Starship girl 74
Sunflowers 18

T

That awful cutter 88
That great black glass 111
The bathroom 60
The chemical estate 50
The exhibit 102
The holy traps 108
The juniper 47
The Light Man 106
The little man 56
The Paxtons 22
The sorry boy from Watertown 58
The sunlit lord 87
The vivid procession 43
The west fields 81
The young poet 75
Those fierce macaws 34
Thoughts at large 44
Throbbing mayapple 41
To the little chickadee 45
Twilit town 61
Two things 82

U

Upon the Monmouth 79

W

What man has to give 113
Which ward? 64

First Line Index

A

Above the world and ours as well 43
A Mid-Atlantic Easter 48
A milky venue laid with lights 102
A morning in the highway seeming sets 106
And at the end there lies nothing but fields 108
And what has man to give upon 113
Another day of carnival 65
As is the unbearable animal 110

B

Beauty in blue and beauty in white—bright 83
Bold youth do year and year again 41
Breakfast 20

C

Can you hear me, Pa? 104
Cassidy! Cassidy! Come to the rood 93
Come rave! Into the garden! 57

D
Does the scientist dare to take the bat 63

E
E'er first cries for authority—which ward? 64
Endless washrooms—young boys in the mirrors 98

F
Father, see your son upright 89
February wastes of dead and gray ground 101
From all illumed and sourceless fell the sun 35
From out the crash, upon the snow 107
From the midnight airstrips, their little lights 99

G
Good morning fairgrounds! Silent fog 16

H
He has them row beneath the sun 90
He is risen 88
High blackened boughs branch through the clay 39
How quiet lies the universe 51

I
I call you mistress, Lesvos 78
In death or a woman I find myself 69
In summer's heat, upon a verdant hill 40
In triple face the goddess gives 37
In wastes of sand forever 105
It rotates through its turns again 34
It's made of reel and ribbon 92
I used to see little figures 42
I used to talk to the bathroom fixtures 60
I was made image of the diamond mind 75

J

Just another night and I am alone 111

K

Kentucky beasts so bridled take the tracks 84

M

Make good on adolescence 59
Man, at the end and dirigible 100
Mary and Mary! Make way! 103
Mary brings a history 28
My love, I'll have the burden 46

N

Nameful, she in many 85

O

October fog again to hide 36
Oh, Father Hux! I have quite forgotten 19
Old professor, his sharp breathing 70
On a young engagement 82
Oy! Starship girl! So far away! 74

R

Remembering remnants of spring—what was 73

S

Safe in some cirque 44
She's lying here, not quite a fairy girl 94
Sudden avatar, real-rendered 26

T

Take care, for civilizations in head 68
The air is thin, more aromatic earth 38
The grand ascent—the gradient! 62
Their concrete is clean 47

Their lives were all of white—no wolven red 61
The lamp set out by mother 25
The last summer lays its twilight softly 23
The little man, he sees it so 56
The night performs its romance 81
The penultimate moment 71
There is but one flitting thing 49
The sorry boy from Watertown 58
The sounds of summer tides accompany 24
The sward as though a city 67
The whole world to their backs, no Dibble House 32
This morning, pregnant with midday, unseen 30
Those brave machines of Switzerland! 72
To fell a like man on even matters 18
To say something of my accolades? 112
To say something of my credentials? 17
To the little chickadee 45
Trial 4-26-573 66

W

Way in those longest fields 87
What dreams are by overcast and autumn 22
What love is of hallucinated kind? 79
Wide fountains with their amaranthine whorls 50
With lissome tones, though by the summer breached 91
With newest ways a boy named Holly comes 86
With white wood still on the Arctic waters 52

Y

Young boy, happy only on the front 53
Young boys with their small papers, criminal 21

Z

Zoe or Zoz 80

Printed in the USA
CPSIA information can be obtained
at www.ICGtesting.com
BVHW030835050923
669009BV00004B/30